some birds some birds, painted and real

most of tea i drink don't have any tea inside,
i follow the packaging and become what they say i will become

arizona in one day and lazy around the back,
those names written with stones around the railway

here, home, the hens are black and small, the donkeys grey and fluffy

home since not that long

i could walk

i don't, framing time with objects

«a man in the box wants to burn my soul» says the song

a mountain after a mountain after a mountain and a man -made- lake,

soon, summer will show up and we will / maybe should we, it would be nice

snow stays up the hill , claiming February power ! to the unconscious birds

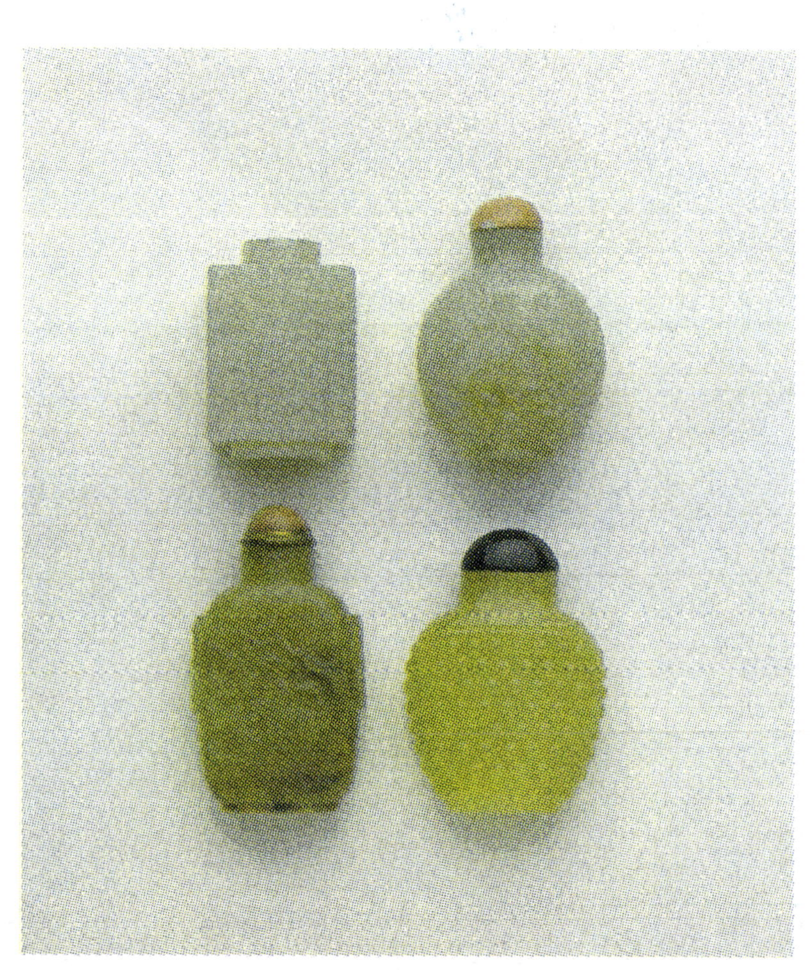

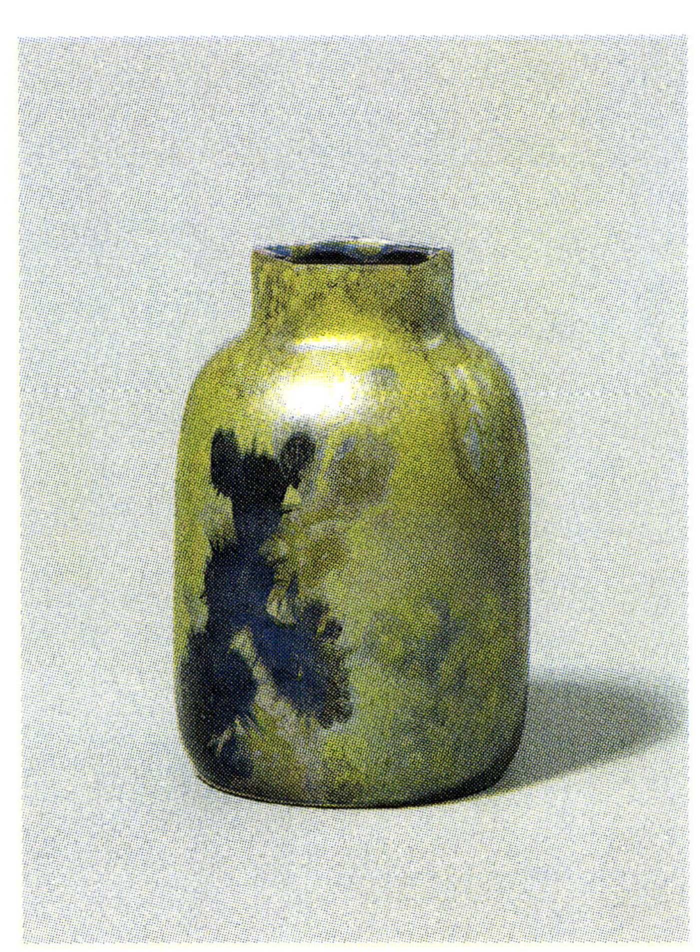

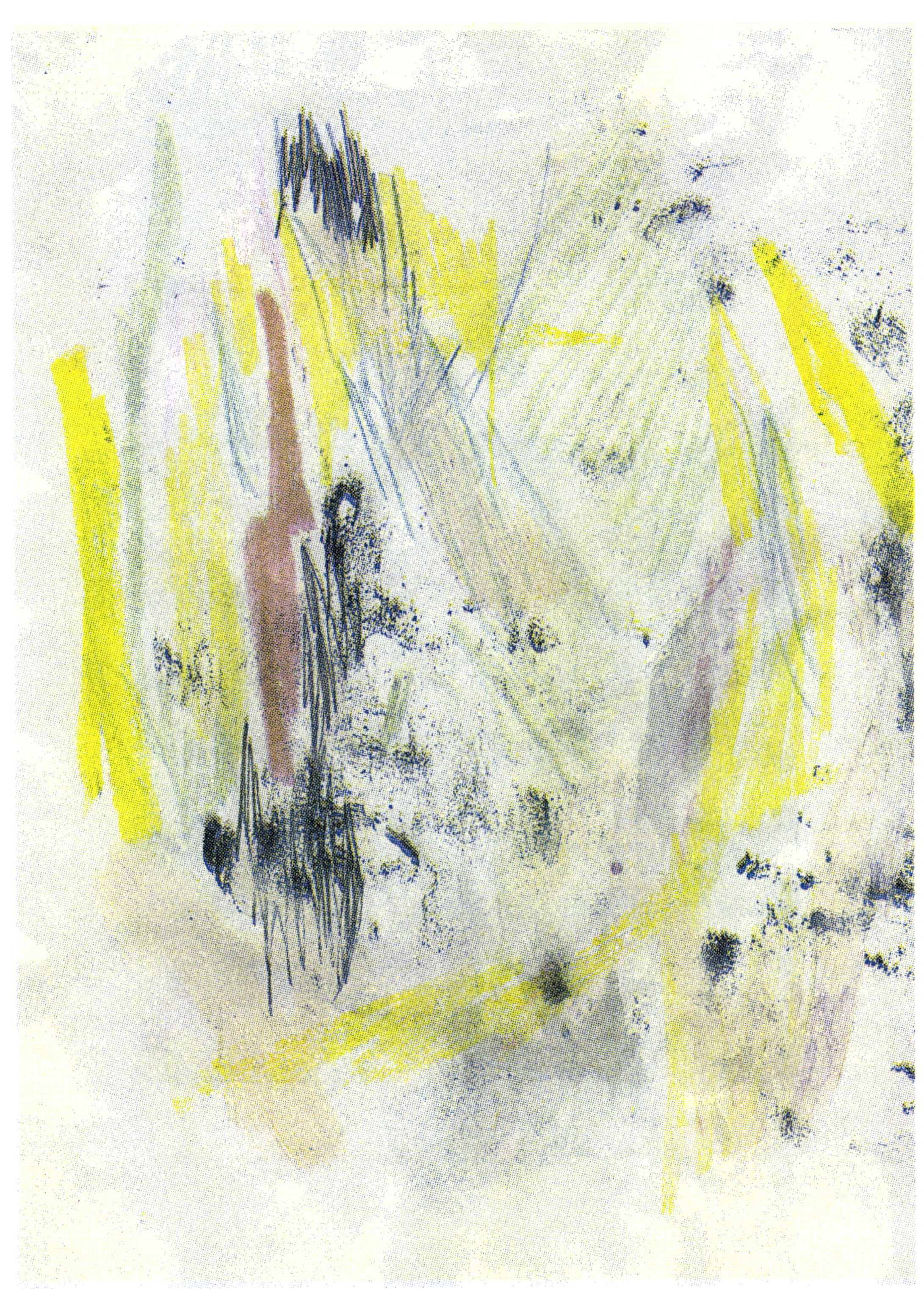

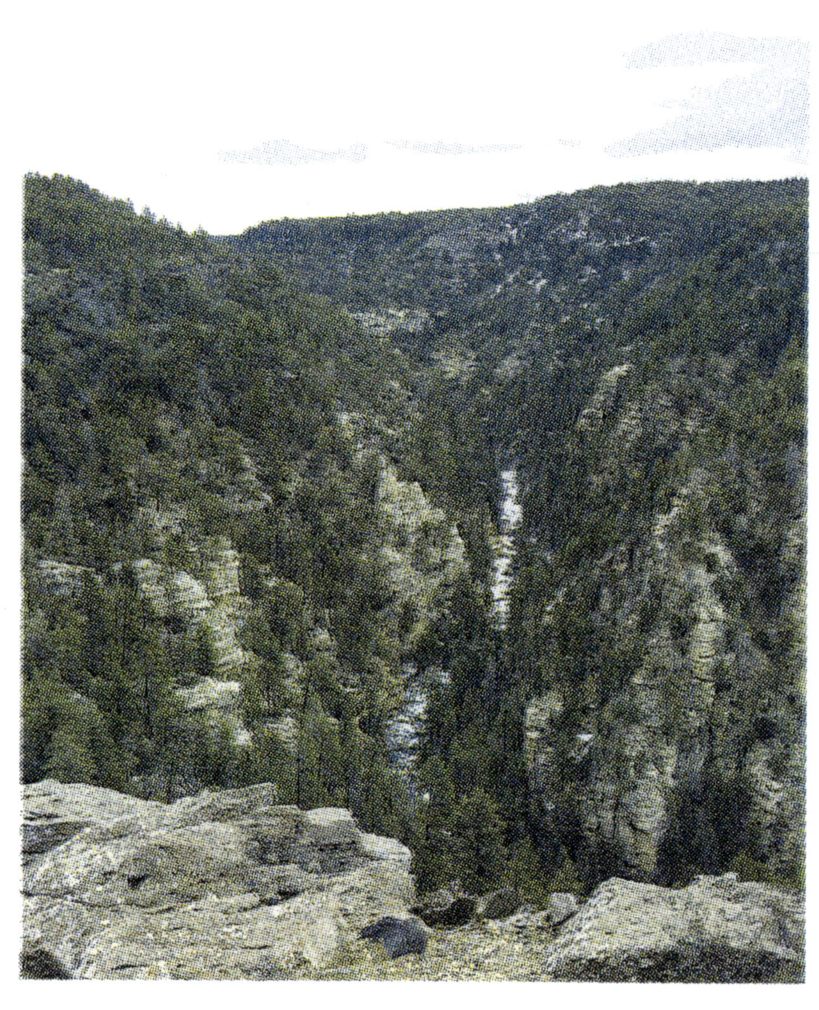

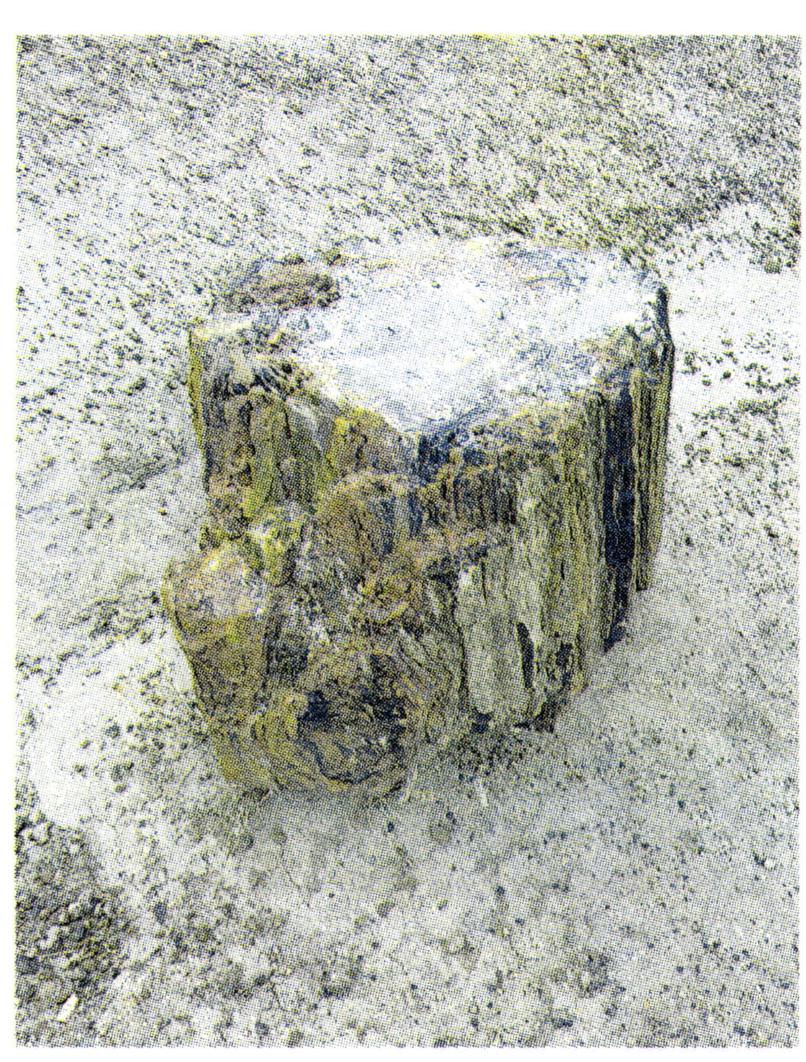

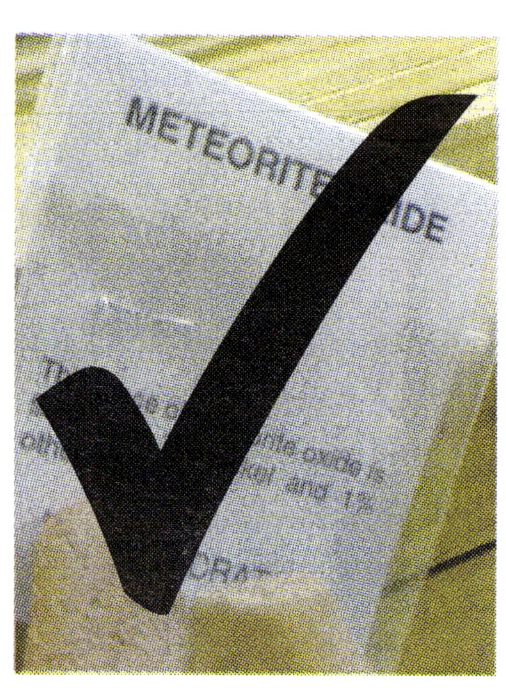
METEORITE

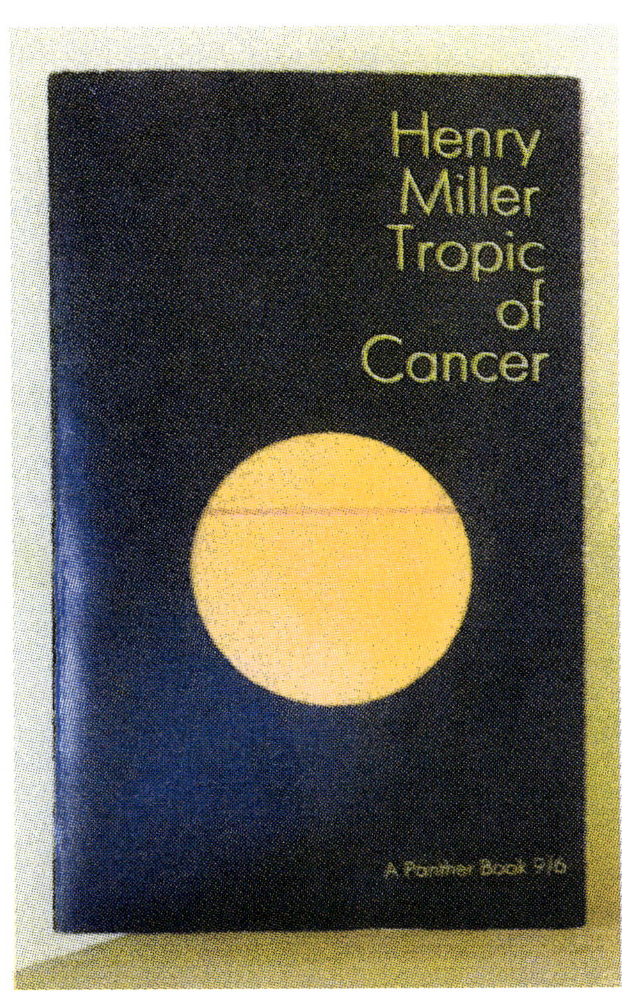
Henry
Miller
Tropic
of
Cancer
A Panther Book 9/6

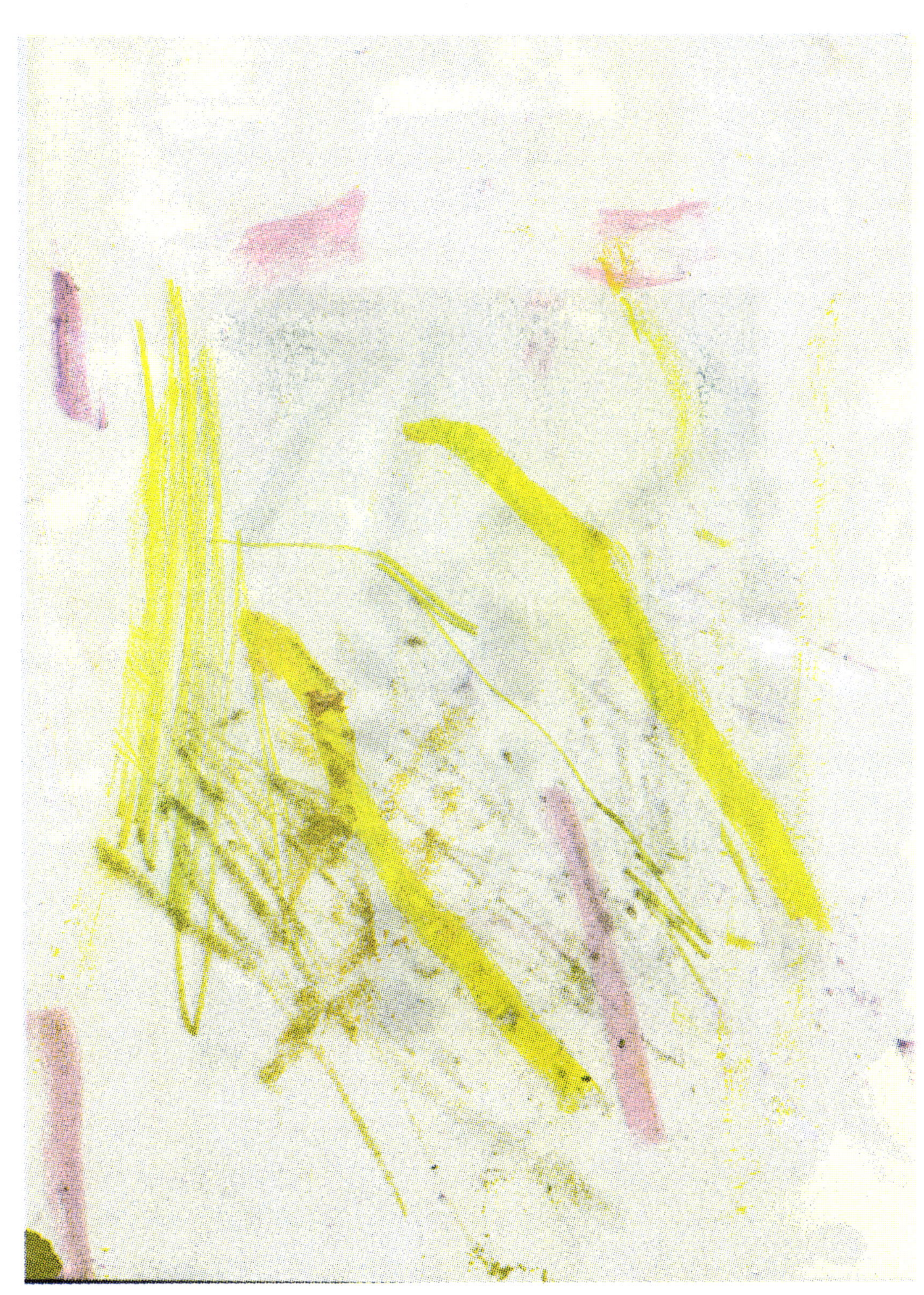

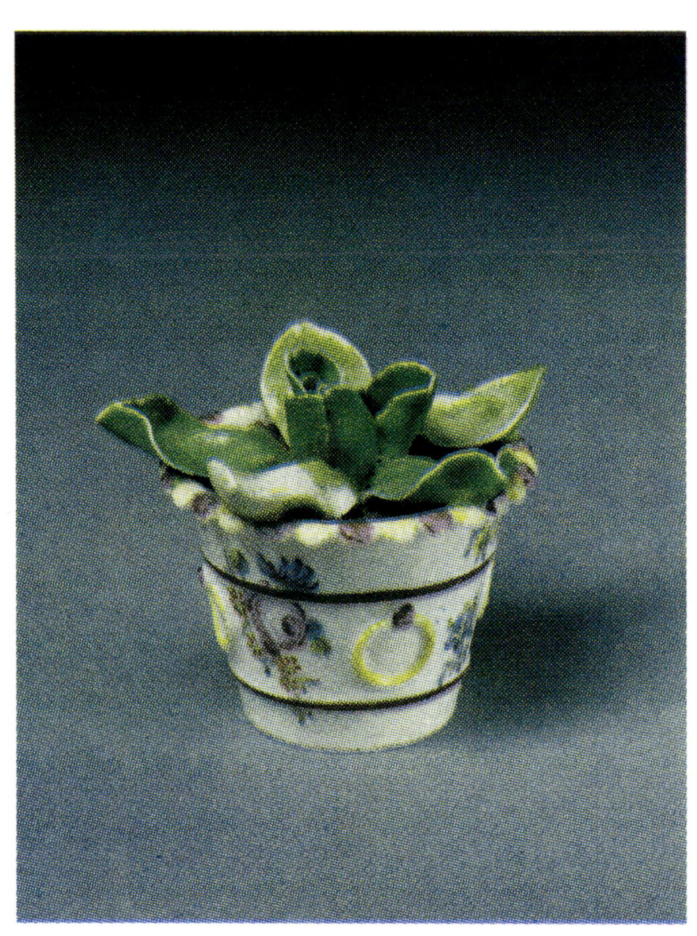

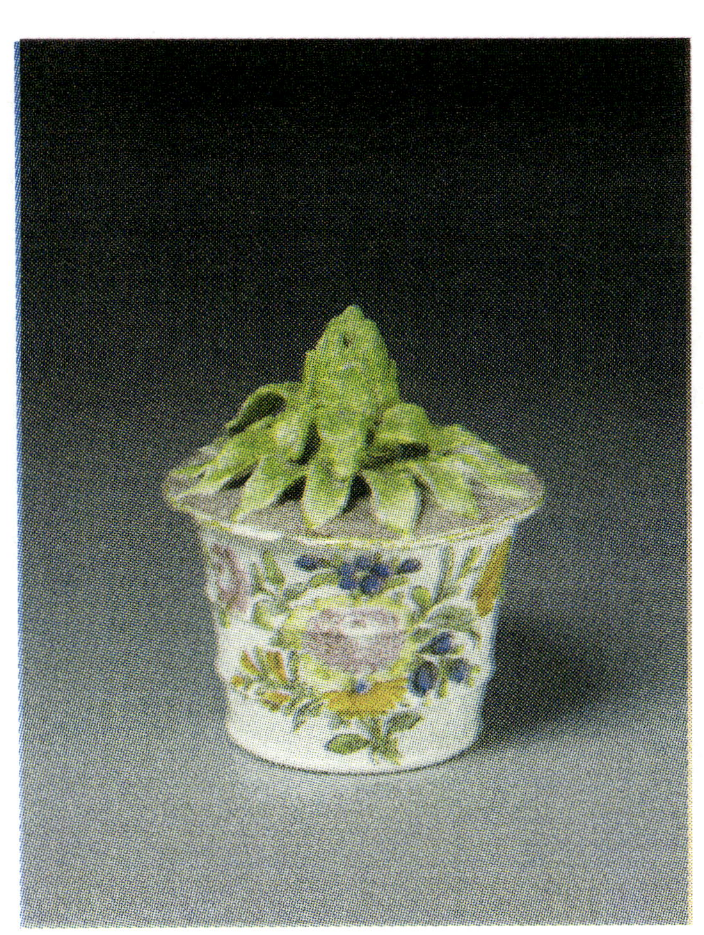

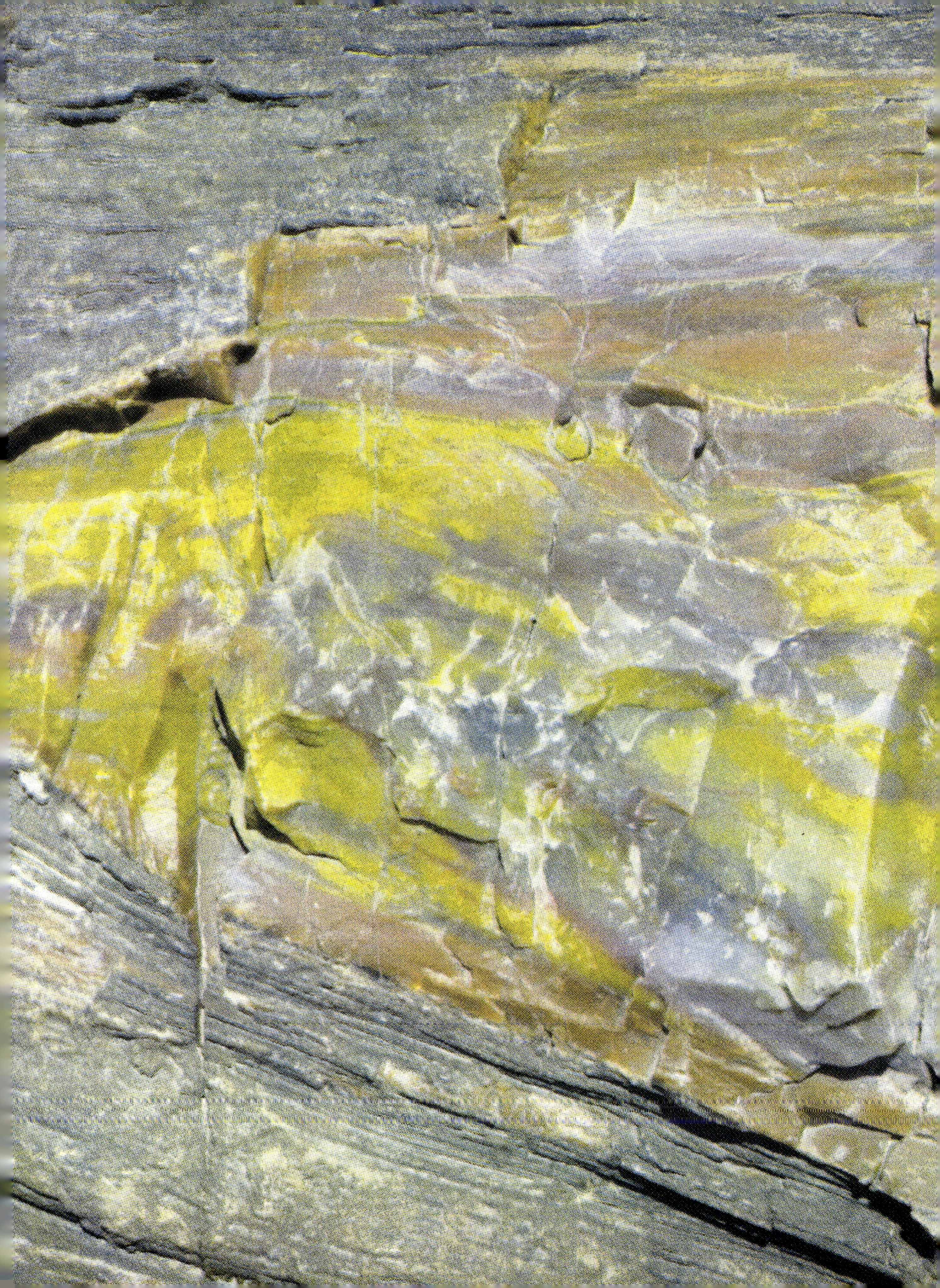

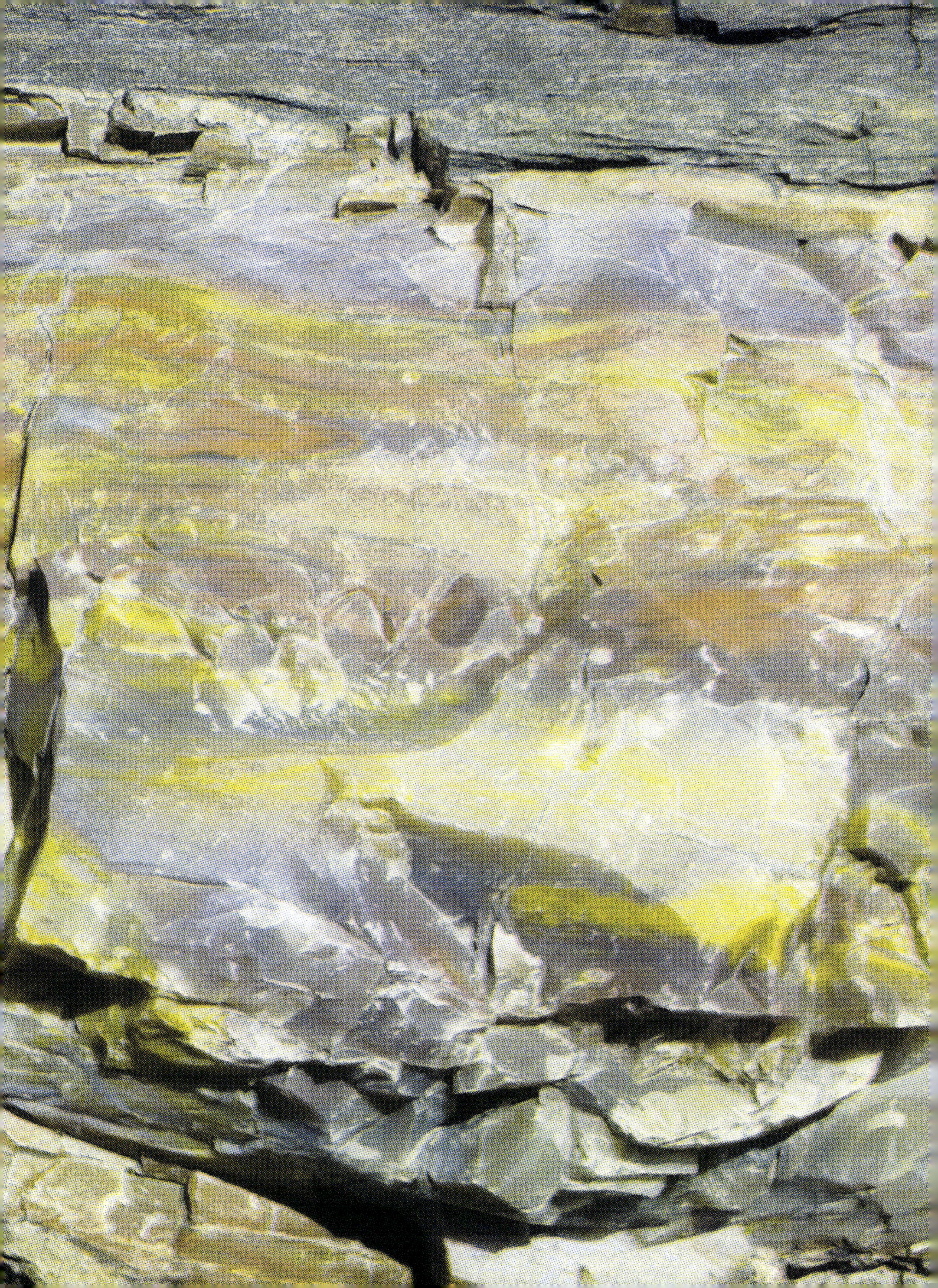

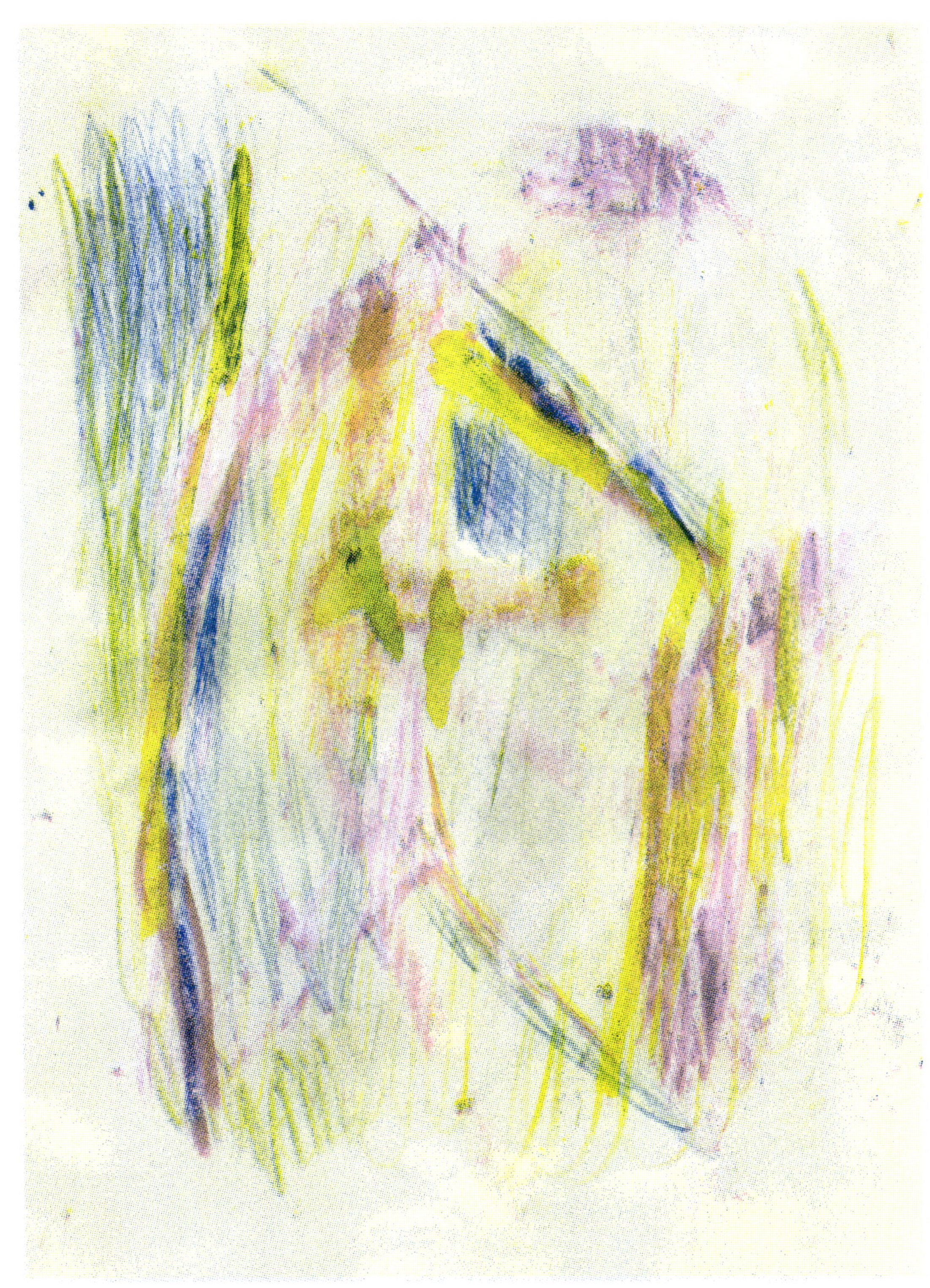

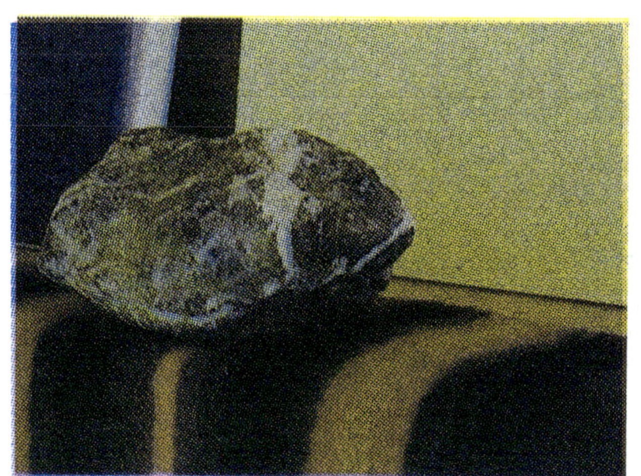

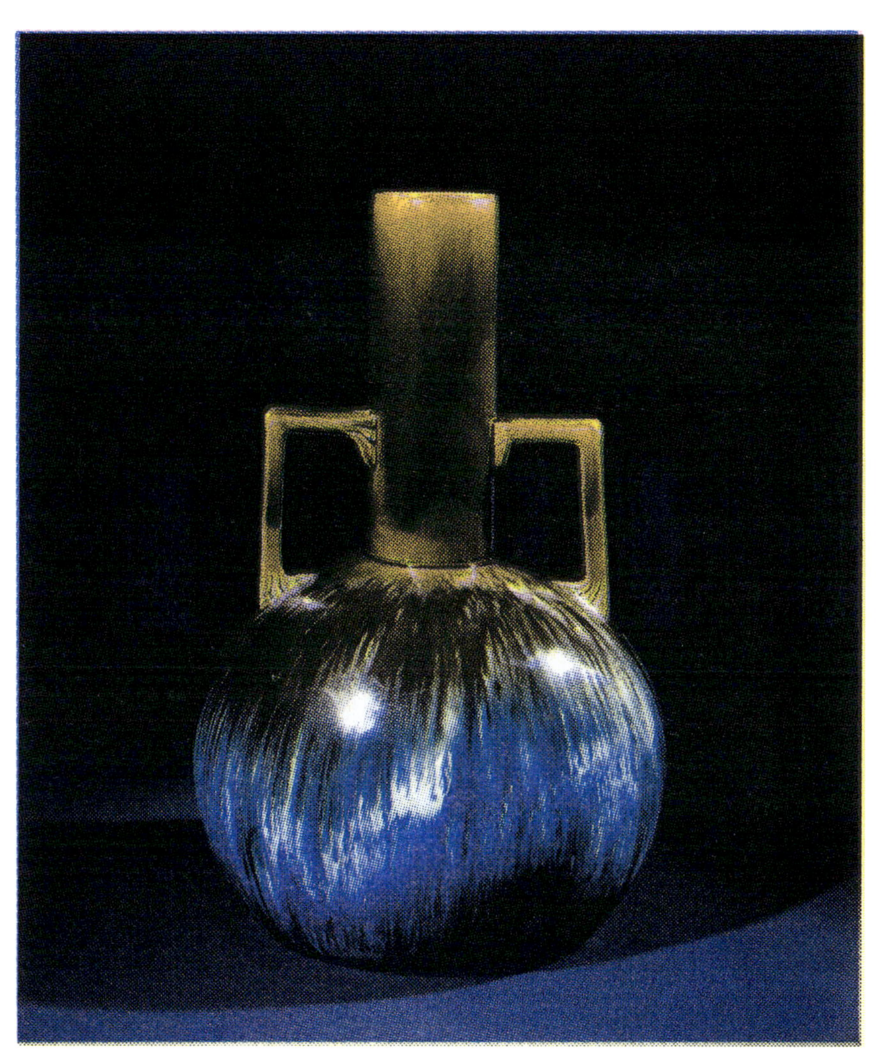

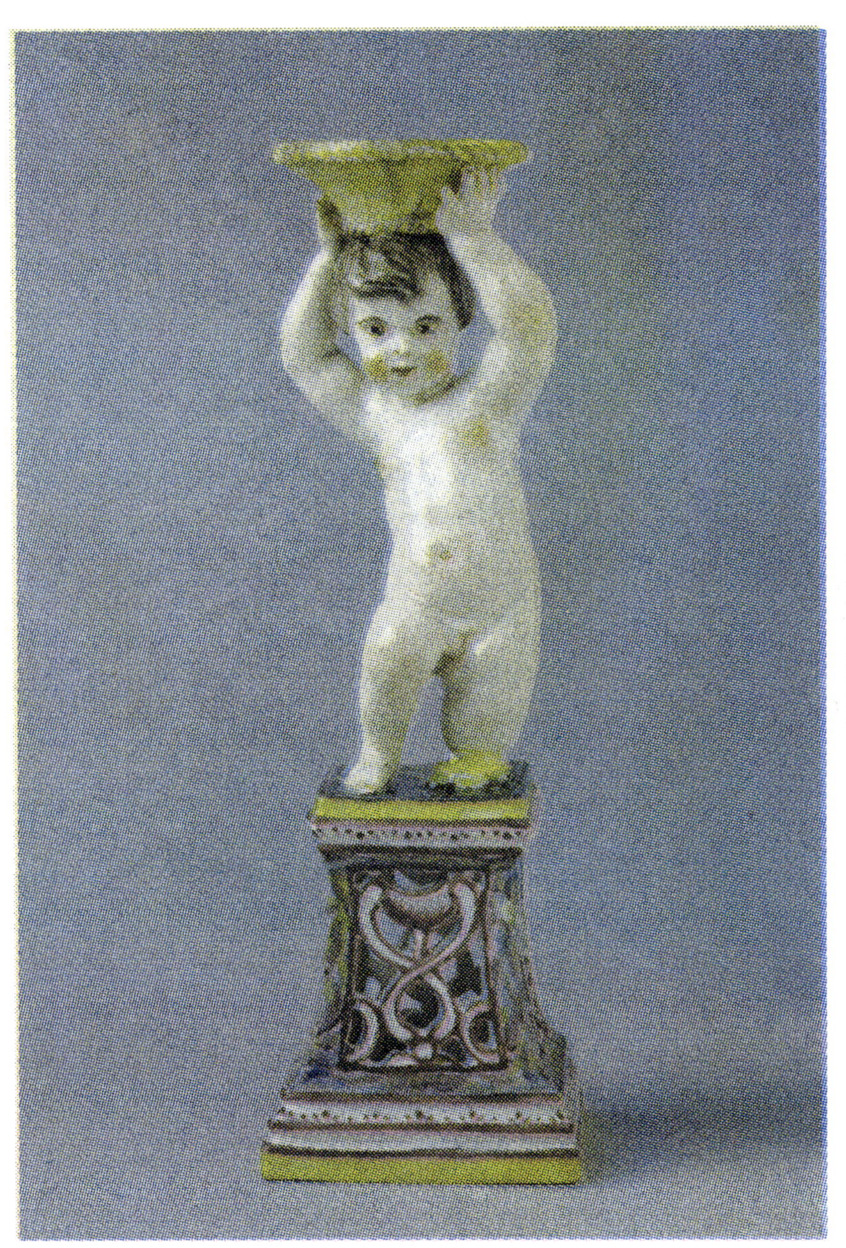

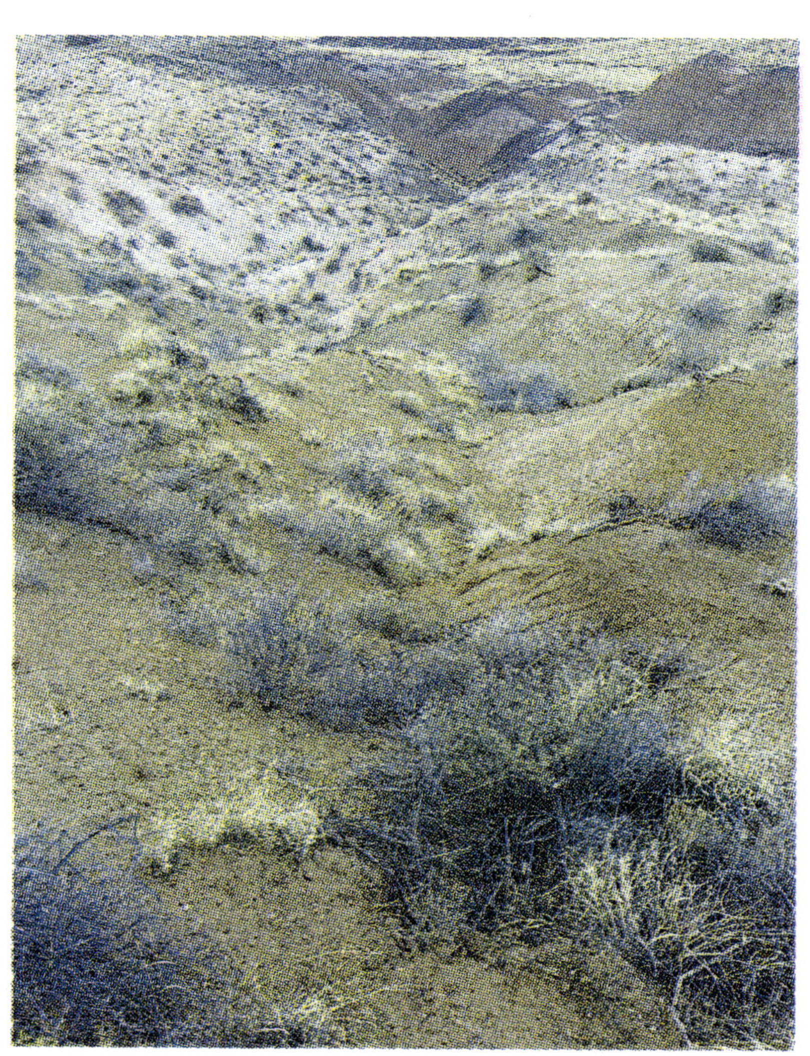

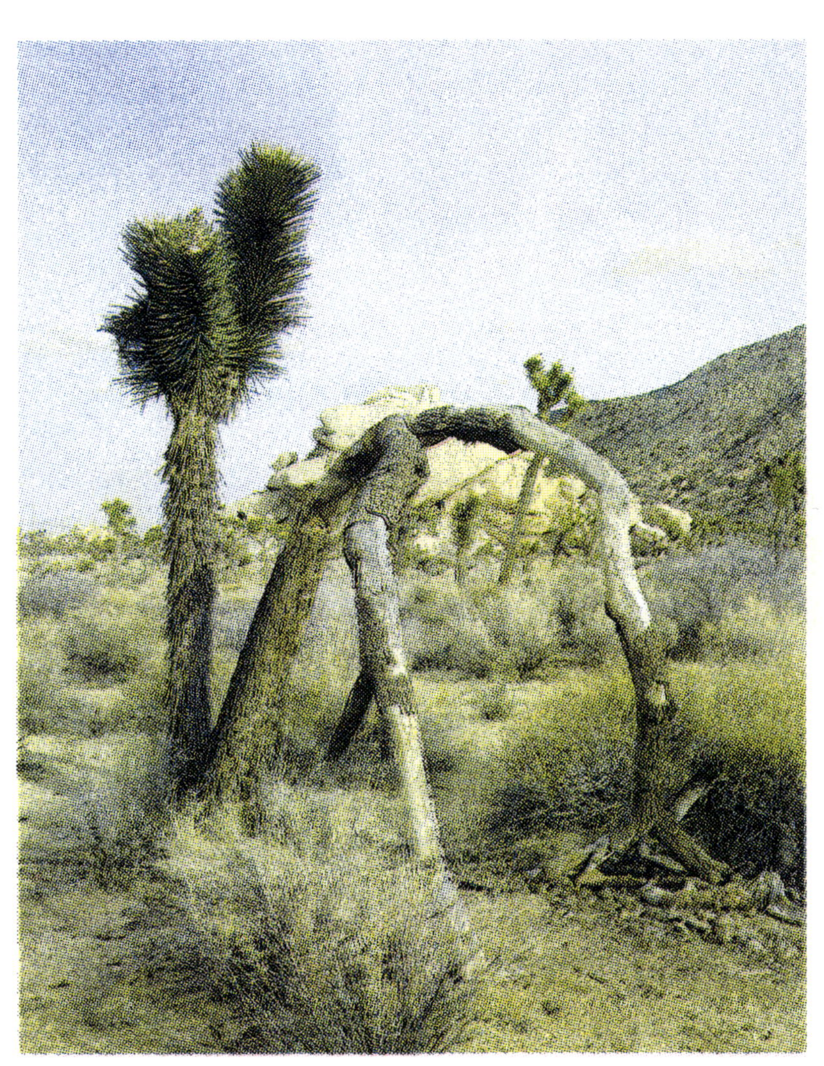

024815

Sagebrush Press

BOOKSTORE

55684 TWENTYNINE PALMS HWY.
YUCCA VALLEY, CALIFORNIA 92284
(E-mail: Sagebrushbooks@verizon.net)
(760) 365-5671

Customer's Order No. | Date 2/4 20 14

Name

Address

Phone:

SOLD BY	CASH	C.O.D.	CHARGE	ON ACCT.	MDSE. RETD.	PAID OUT	LAYAWAY
Frank	✓						

QUAN.	DESCRIPTION	PRICE	AMOUNT
4	Post cards		1.00
	Guidebook to the Colorado River	Bx	5.50
	Part I + Part 2	Bx	7.50
	Koalas Live Here / Eberle	–	5.00
Magazine	Child Life / June July 1955		4.50
	The Grade Teacher Jan 1954		4.00
	Sports Afield / Aug 1953		2.00
	Desert Mag. Jan. 1969		3.00
Petrified Forest	ARIZona Hwy / May 1948		10.00
			42.50

All claims and returned goods MUST be accompanied by this bill.

TAX	3.40
TOTAL	$45.90

Received By

GSCC 650-2
PRINTED IN U.S.A.

Thank You

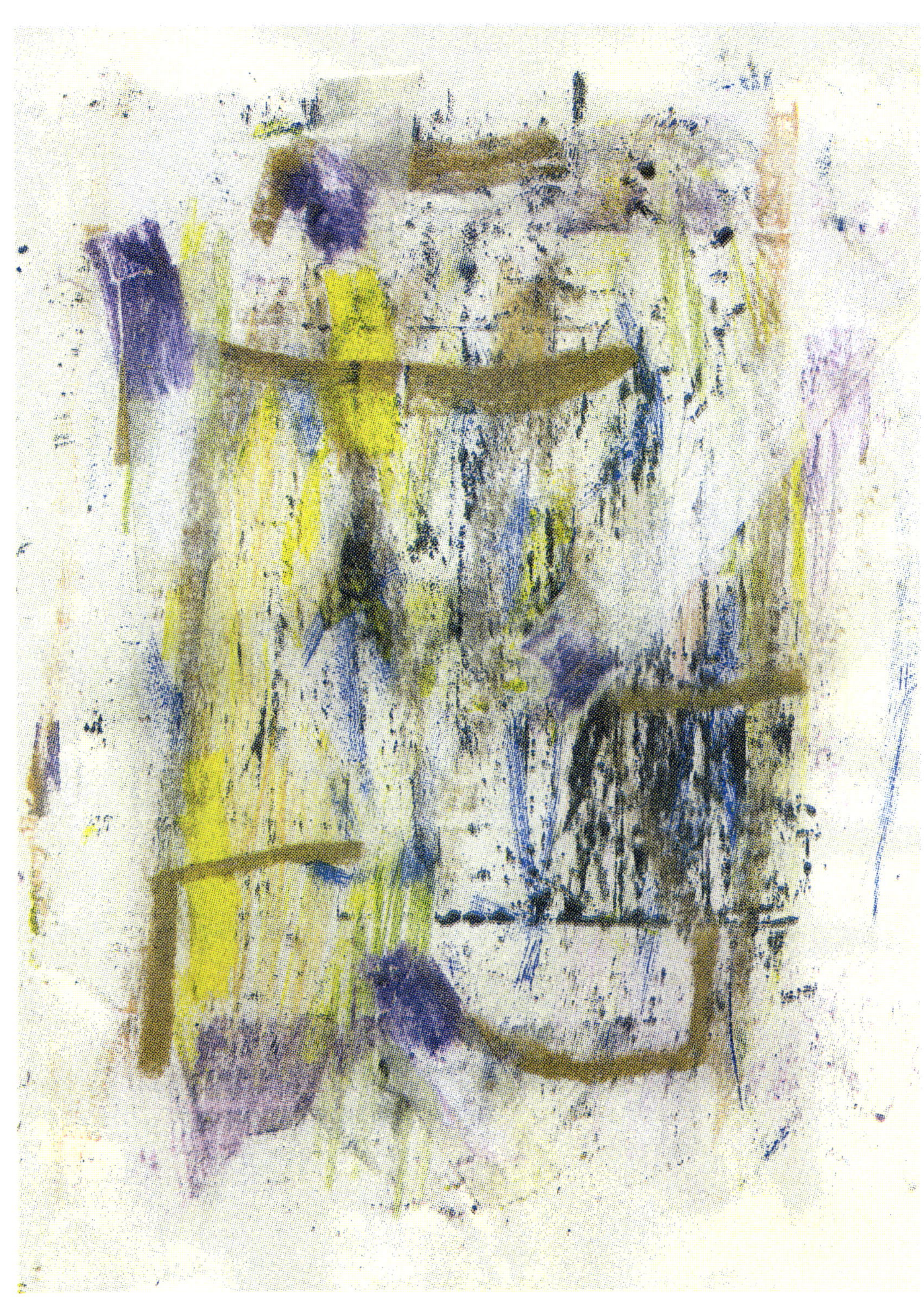

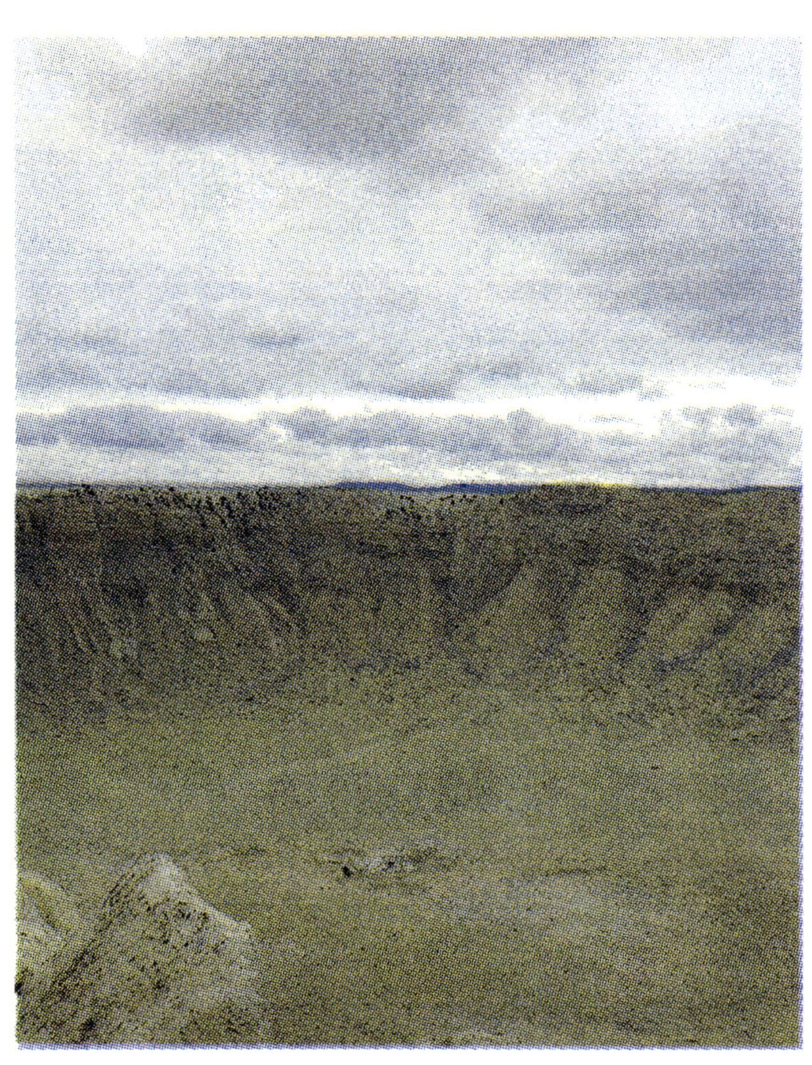

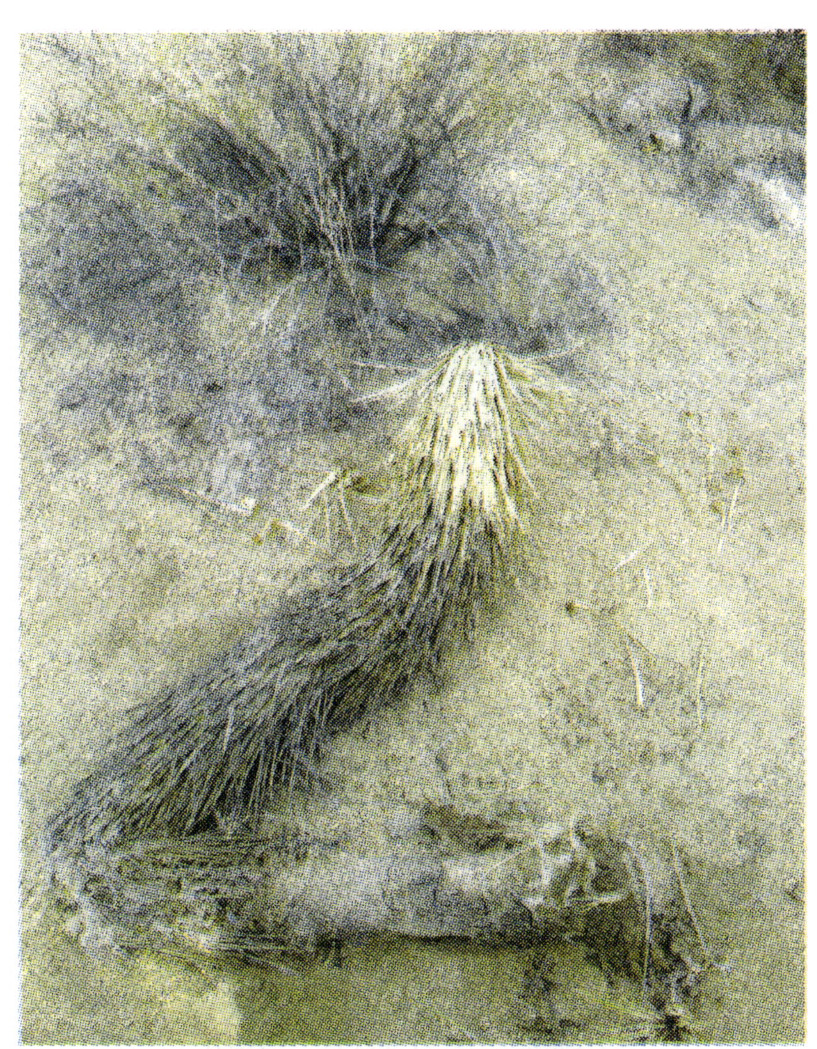

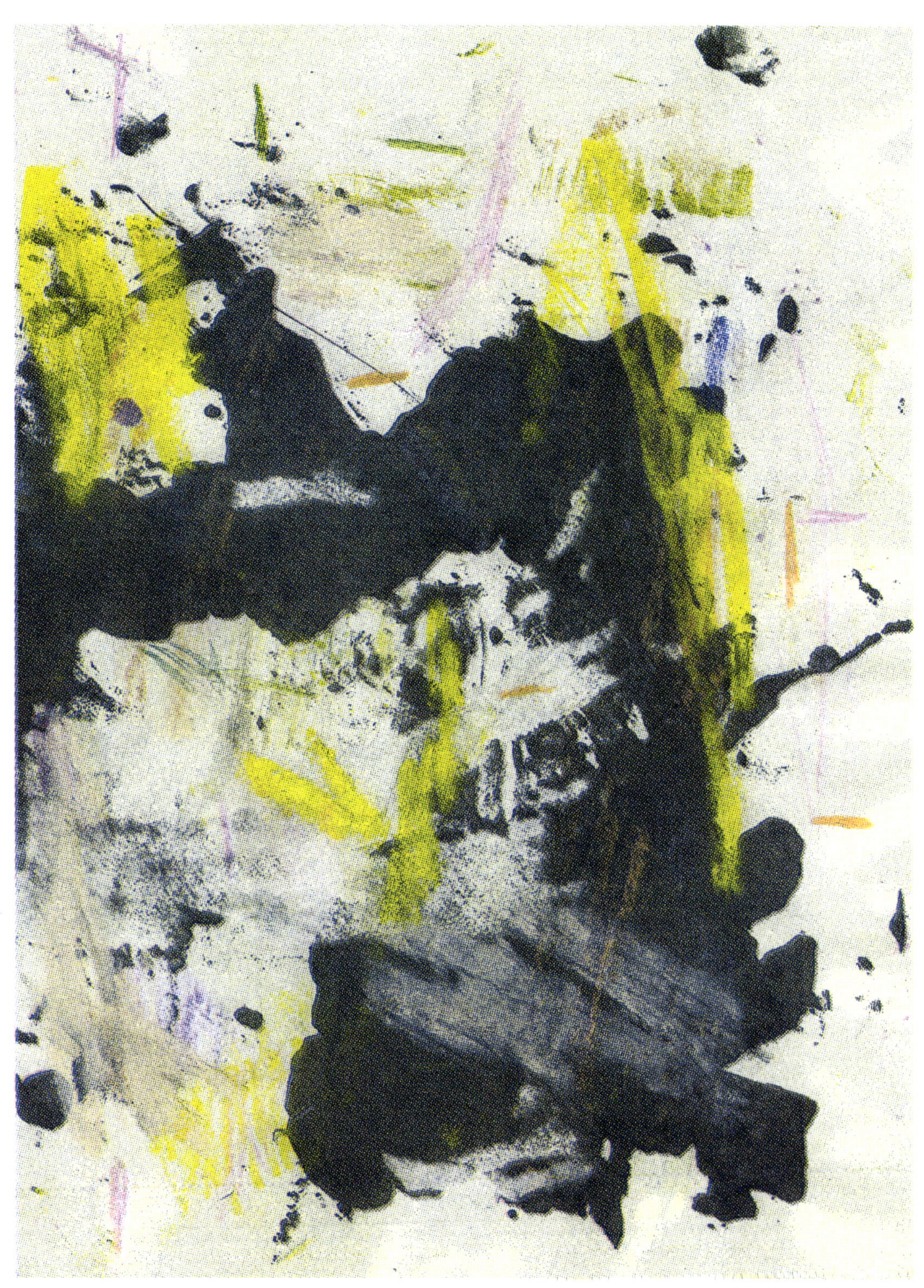